SURVIVING
THE STORM

❖

poems by
Patrick W. Flanigan, M.D.

illustrations by
Christine Crozier

Pacific Grove Publishing

Graphic design: Mark Ryan

Printed in the United States of America
by Cypress Lithographics, Monterey, California

Published by:
Pacific Grove Publishing
P.O. Box 803
Pacific Grove, CA 93950
Telephone: (831) 424-2866
FAX: (831) 375-4749

1 3 5 7 6 4 2

ISBN 0-9668952-3-1

In memory of my mother,
Leona V. Flanigan.

CONTENTS

LISTEN

Have you ever heard
a muffled voice
like a cry for help
coming from the rubble
of a collapsed building?

Have you ever stopped,
put down the newspaper,
turned off the television,
gone into the garden
and just listened?

Sitting quietly,
you might be able
to hear the voice
more clearly.
You might be able
to rescue the soul
buried under the weight
of daily routine.

WAIT

Wait for the seed buried
in the rain soaked soil
to sprout,
to struggle against gravity,
to reach toward the sun,
to bear fruit in the fall.

Wait for the egg in the nest
to silently rest, carefully tended
until gentle tapping from inside
grows in intensity,
until there is a crack
and a tiny blind chick emerges
to be fed, to grow,
and to fly.

Wait for the baby,
product of seed and egg,
to build arms and legs,
head and hands,
to kick against nourishing
but restraining womb,
to tunnel into the sunlight
screaming,
to change from tiny infant,
to toddler, to teen, to adult.

Wait for your own soul,
unseen and often forgotten,
to grow inside your skin,
to read, to listen,
to feel
until suddenly
it shines forth
in colors yet unknown.

PATIENCE

Some things cannot be rushed—
the appearance of a shooting star,
the opening of a flower,
the growth of a child,
a marriage that lasts.

I do not know how these things happen—
where that blaze of fire in the sky started,
what compelled that plant to bloom,
what turned that tiny baby into a woman,
why you stayed with me all these years.

I do know that these things cannot be rushed.
They happen at their own pace
and are seen only by those
patient enough to wait
and lucky enough to be there.

FOR MY WIFE

She wanted me
to write a poem
about her.

But she was warm sunshine,
soul lifting laughter,
a gypsy dance,
breathless love,
a calm voice on a stormy night,
wise counsel in a confusing world.

Who could write
a poem
about all of that?

FAIRY DANCE

Sometimes light
dances on the water
like thousands of fairies
celebrating the wedding
of the sun and the moon.

Constantly moving,
silently laughing,
fleet-footed revelers
remind us
to live and rejoice.

Farther off shore
giant whales
spout white plumes
of hot breath
and sing for us all.

THE LOVE POEM

He started to write
a love poem
on the petals
of a daisy.

Not knowing
if she loved him
or loved him not,
he dared

to expose his soul
like the yellow
gold center of the flower
on which he wrote.

Before black ink
stained the last white petal,
she touched his neck
and whispered "I love you."

THE BRIDE

Gay ribbons
of white and pink and rose
streamed from her hair and wrists
and her flowing satin dress
flashed in the sunlight
as she danced
through the green meadow
and ancient orchard.

New grass,
still virginal and without seed,
welcomed her bare feet
as she moved
like a bird, like a butterfly,
like a pixie
among the yellow mustard flowers
growing in spring profusion.

The young yellow-green leaves of the trees
peeked at her shyly
as they hid
among the thousands of white blossoms.
The dark tree trunks and branches,
made even darker by the recent shower,
seemed mute and in awe
as she skipped and twirled
to the music of the lark.

Distant clouds fled
from her movement and joy,
leaving behind
blue sky and a rainbow.

THE FLOWERING TREE

In my garden
a certain tree
blooms every summer.
It does not
bear fruit
but covers itself
with more flowers
than there are
numbers in the world.
Its joy and generosity
are amazing—
to produce
such beauty
and not have
eyes.

SCENTS

The honeysuckle sent
its fragrant perfume
through the crack under the door
awakening him just after dawn.

The garden sought his attention
seducing him
to sink his strong hands
into its moist soil.

He sang softly
gently trimming
and caressing leaves
and stems and blooms.

He worked until dusk
returning to his room,
the scents of a thousand flowers
on his skin.

THE GREEN OF SPRING

After months of rain
everything seems new,
fragile, and green.
Blades of grass
cover the meadow,
yellow-green leaves
adorn the trees,
green buds
swell atop stems,
the brick path
is mossy and slick.

But the bark
of the ancient oaks,
pines, and cypress
are not new,
fragile, or green.
They are creviced and wrinkled,
scarred and rough.
They are the brown color
of the rich, moist earth
that, each year,
gives birth
to the bright green
of springtime.

THE VISIT

A sad man visited the garden
but the color of its blooms,
the perfume in the air,
the antics of the hummingbird
overwhelmed his grief
and he laughed.

FOG

Some mornings are very quiet.

Fog obscures color and detail,
muffles sounds,
keeps birds in their nests,
whispers "stay in bed."

It bathes plants and earth,
bejewels spider webs,
moistens rose buds,
silences footsteps.

Fog quietly delivers its message:
move softly,
love gently,
accept mystery.

THE BASIN

A metal basin
full of water,
smooth surfaced
and quiet,
sits on the rocky bank
of a dancing,
babbling stream.

"Come play,"
calls the stream.
"Just be,"
whispers the basin.

SAND AND PEBBLES

Unyielding boulders
make the water
twist and tumble
as it travels
from the mountains
to the sea.
In quiet pools
along the stream
sand and smooth pebbles
silently bear witness
to the wisdom of the water,
the power of persistence,
and the inevitability of change.

THE WALL

Smooth stones
freed from
mountainous boulders
ages ago,
rough edges
tumbled away
on the shores
of primordial lakes,
are once again
held together
by concrete
working as one
to form a wall
in a garden
by a pond
with green lily pads
and tiny golden fish.

SUNFLOWERS

Sunflowers are the giants of the garden.
They watch the movement of the field mouse
and the flight of the sparrow.
They breathe the heavy perfume
of the honeysuckle and jasmine.
They hear the hum of the bee
and the soft singing of the gardener.

They know more than all the other plants
in the summer garden.
This knowledge, turning into wisdom,
makes them bow their massive heads.

THE COAST

Nervous little birds
dart across the face
of a seaside cliff.

Endless waves
roll and foam
rattling the rocks below.

A black cat with no tail
stretches in the
sunlit garden above.

Life moves and sings
out of the great silence
all around.

IN A SMALL ROOM

Once, in a small room,
I saw Christ.
He did not walk in
with a beard and white robe.

He walked in
with earth colored skin
wrinkled by years
working in the sun
on the farms
of California, Oregon,
and Washington.

He walked in
wearing tattered clothes,
bearing the burden
of a serious illness,
and holding the hand
of a loving daughter.

He owned little.

I did not recognize Him
until He smiled.

Now I look carefully
at every face
and study every smile,
even the one I see
in the mirror.

ON EASTER SUNDAY

On Easter Sunday
we gather
to worship a man
killed by a crowd
2,000 years ago.

That ancient crowd
was eager to kill
to protect belief
and prevent blasphemy.

If we had been there
seeing His gentle face
and hearing His command
to love one another,
would we have tried
to save Him?

You may know
what you
would have done.
I worry that I
might have stood
with the priests,
the proud, the pious
and shouted
"Crucify Him!"

CALIFORNIA POPPIES

The poppies
on the face
of the rocky cliff
glow
like a fire.

Their bright petals
are smooth and soft
like the lips
of a lover.

Their thin leaves
are delicate
like fragile lace
made years ago
by the patient hands
of wives
waiting on shore
for their seafaring husbands
to return from months
on distant seas.

The poppies
on the dry cliff
prove
that sometimes
seeds fall
on rocky, barren ground
and thrive,
surviving
because of their pure
love of life.

THIS LIFE

The bookstore shelves
are full of books
about past lives
and out of body experiences.

How lucky those authors
must be
to know so much
and have lived so long.

I struggle each day
hardly able to live
this life
and experience this body.

Maybe tomorrow
I will look in the mirror
and see
Julius Caesar or St. Francis

but today
I am content
to see a face
that simply needs a shave.

TOUCHING THE HORIZON

Surrounded by high walls,
seeing only sky
above stones and mortar,
I reach up
and touch the top of the wall.

Have I touched the Horizon?

Can God be far away?

GRANDPA'S PIPE

Grandpa smoked a pipe.

He could hold
a six year old boy
on his lap,
pick up his pipe,
tap out the ash,
scrape the bowl clean,
blow through the stem
until it whistled,
open a leather pouch,
refill the pipe,
tamp down
the sweet smelling tobacco,
and light it with a match

all the while saying
you are a fine, beloved boy
without speaking a word.

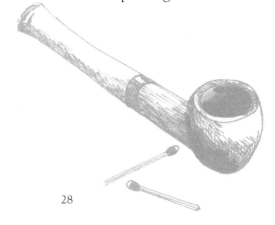

AUTUMN

When autumn comes
and leaves change
from green to brown,
when chill enters the night,
when wrinkles creep
across hands and face
like weeds grown
in the summer sun,
when people no longer say
you look so young,
will I remember
the soft sound of spring rain,
the crash of thunder,
the song of the redbird,
the music of your voice?

WELL WORN

Most of my things
do not acquire a patina
even though I like
faded jeans,
well worn leather,
and the muted green
of weathered copper.

Maybe I wash my hands
too often
and touch the world around me
too little.

I remember outgrowing
a cowboy outfit as a child.
It was as clean as new
when we gave it away.

Time is making me
less afraid
of scars and stains,
more appreciative
of the hard and soft
people and things
around me,
more willing
to risk everything
to be well worn
and pleasantly used
before I outgrow
this life.

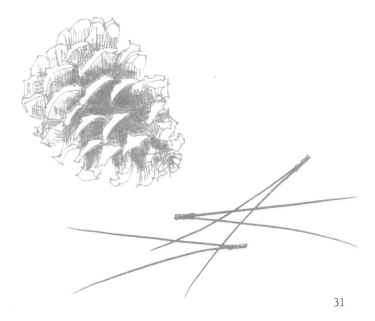

THE PIANO

A beloved daughter
sitting at the piano
reached into her memory
and her soul
to bring forth music
once played only by angels.

You rested on the couch
holding my hand.
We cried in joy and sorrow,
knowing this moment
would never come again.

ABOVE THE STORM

The winter storm
lashed the coast
all night.
Large rocks,
too heavy
for ten men
to lift,
rolled and clattered
in the waves.
The wind howled
through frantic trees.

Above the tumult
I heard
your cry of pain
from a thousand miles away.

I felt heavier
than the bedrock
beneath the sea.
I could not move
as salt tears
mixed with the rain.

DISTANCE

We measure distance
in so many ways –
inches, miles, light years –
and yet I do not know how
to measure the distance
between two people
sitting side by side
silent
or talking about the weather.

Hurt and history
keep them apart.
Blood and history
keep them together,
but always
between them is a distance
impossible to measure,
impossible to ignore.

THE VETERAN

The longest train
I ever saw
puffed black smoke
and hissed white steam
as it carried you
away from your youth,
your innocence,
and me.

You returned
with a limp,
tobacco and whiskey
on your breath,
nervous eyes,
and a heart
that gave out
at thirty nine.

Fifty years later
I still avoid train stations
and hate the harsh sounds
of steel wheels on steel rails
and the howl of whistles
in the night.

THE OAK

An oak tree stood on the hillside years ago
when covered wagons
first rolled onto the floor of the valley
as native peoples
watched the new arrivals with wonder.
That same oak toppled today
in a gentle breeze.
No more than a sigh
brought it to the ground
with a crash and a groan.

Will the birds that nested in its branches,
the squirrels that feasted on its acorns,
and the shy lovers who kissed
and grew bold in its shade
miss the oak as much as I miss you?

DRIFTWOOD

The bleached trunk
of a once tall tree
rests on a rocky shore
beneath a cliff
topped by cypress
and redwoods.

Months in storm tossed seas
and encounters
with other shores
have stripped away
bark and branches
leaving bare wood,
white and smooth.

The trees above whisper
about the skeleton below.
Some raise their boughs
to heaven in fear and trembling.
Others simply enjoy
the sky, the moist earth,
and the birds
nesting in their branches.

THE FIRE

The faint red of dawn
quietly came upon the city
only to be broken
by the red flash of the lights
and the red mass of the fire engine
moving toward the parted
scream-filled red lips
of the woman kneeling,
hands pulling her own
tinted red hair,
beside the bloodied
red body of a boy
lying beside a burning
red building
and a red, red rose.

YOUR DEATH

Your death
was not a simple fact:
body temperature, weight,
hair color, dimensions.
It changed lives
like a siren drives away silence.

Your death
haunted those who found you,
fed nightmares,
distorted familiar things,
made me aware
of what still lives.

GRIEF

Don't talk to me of grief.

I have seen
the red-rimmed eyes
of a sister
who spent all night
talking to her brother
dying of leukemia.

I have touched
the sagging sad shoulders
of a father
who stood twelve hours praying for his child
lying in a coma.

I have looked
at the lost lonely face
in the mirror
shaving while you
return to the dust
of our origins.

I know there is
salve for wounds,
comfort for loss,
hope of reunion.

But let's not talk about that now.

SURVIVING THE STORM

How do they do it?
How do dolphins and great whales
survive through night long storms
when white capped waves
cover the ocean from horizon to horizon,
when spray fills the air,
when rain pours down in solid sheets?

How do they suck air
into their huge lungs without drowning
in the water all around them?

They must know the secrets that we know.
They must know the secrets that help us
smile and breathe and survive
without drowning in the sorrow all around us.

They must be able to
see the beauty of a raindrop,
hear the song of the wind,
feel their belonging to the universe.

ON MOTHER'S DAY

On Mother's Day
the cemetery is a lively place.

Flowers, balloons, a blue and white Teddy bear
adorn the graves.
Children in suits and dresses
scamper and laugh.
Families and friends
cluster around this grave
and that one over there.
A greyhaired man
carrying roses
stumbles
walking alone
toward a piece of granite
that says
Wife, Mother, Friend.

And I sit here
on a stone bench
looking at your name
and fresh cut tulips
hoping that you can see
the flowers,
your son,
and the love he has for you.

CHANTING

The chanting of the monks
droned on and on.
The Latin phrases
and simple melodies
pushed out thoughts
of work and toil.
Money seemed irrelevant.
Distinctions between
friend and foe
disappeared.

Voices blended
and bounced off
the stone walls
of the ancient chapel.
Light filtered through
stained glass windows
tinting tiny dust specks
hovering in the vibrating,
sound drenched air
blue, red, purple.

Hearts, breath, every atom
moved in harmony
with the music,
moved out of time
and out of space.

Briefly the veil parted,
illusion faded
revealing the Unity
and Mystery
some call God.

THE ONLY CHOICE

The only choice
is to open
like leaves unfurling
in spring,
like flowers blooming
in summer,
like a hungry baby
seeking the breast,
like a voice
parting clenched teeth
and riding
on the wind
over the earth.

The withering
that comes in fall,
the closing of the eyes and mouth
in the tomb,
these are not choices.
These come
to the patient
and the impatient alike.

Only the voice
still echoes
after the mouth
is closed.
Only the voice
remains
if we choose
to open.

BENEATH THE SNOW

During the darkest winter night
slumbering beneath the snow
seeds and bulbs wait
for the windsong of spring

that will awaken them
to sink deep roots
and send leaves and buds
toward the sun.

I know this to be true
not because I have
shoveled away the snow
or dug into the frozen earth

but because I have watched
the wheel of time spinning on its axis
and because I believe the ancient voices
that proclaimed for everything there is a season.

ISBN 0-9668952-3-1